DATE DUE

S0-EPV-099

TIVERTON BRANCH	TIVERTON BRANCH
NOV 8 RECD	DEC 9 4 RECD
DEC 16 1989	DEC 22 1995
DEC 23 1989	DEC 24 1998
DEC 15 1990	Jan 4, 2000
JAN -8 1991	DEC 15 2000
	BCPL-CH 11/02
DEC 17 1991	JAN 10 2003
JAN -9 1991	DEC 18 2003
	DEC 16 2004
JAN -5 1992	TA 1/07
DEC 18 RECD	
JAN 11 1996	
DEC 12 1996	
FEB 11 1999	

J394.268282
Chi
(6)

BRUCE COUNTY PUBLIC LIBRARY
P.O. BOX 16000
PORT ELGIN, ONTARIO
N0H 2C0

A CHILD'S BOOK OF Christmas

Designed by Patrick T. McRae

IDEALS CHILDREN'S BOOKS
Nashville, Tennessee

ACKNOWLEDGMENTS

CHRISTMAS SONG from *COMPLETE POEMS BY EUGENE FIELD,* published by Charles Scribner's Sons; OUR LADY'S JUGGLER by Anatole France, published by Dodd, Mead & Company, Inc.; THE FRIENDLY BEASTS, arrangement copyright © 1954 Augsburg Publishing House. Reprinted by permission from *CAROLS FOR CHRISTMAS;* OLD SPANISH CAROL from *THE LONG CHRISTMAS* by Ruth Sawyer. Copyright 1941, renewed © by Ruth Sawyer. All rights reserved. Reprinted by permission of Viking Penguin Inc.; Our sincere thanks to the following whose addresses we were unable to locate: Joan Ashurst for THE PRANCING TOYS; Alice Leedy Mason for SOME ABC'S OF CHRISTMAS.

Copyright © MCMLXXXVIII by Ideals Publishing Corporation.
All rights reserved.
Printed and bound in the United States of America.
Published by Ideals Publishing Corporation
Nelson Place at Elm Hill Pike
Nashville, Tennessee 37214

ISBN 0-8249-8274-6

Table of Contents

ABC'S OF CHRISTMAS 8
THE TOYS OF CHRISTMAS
    Greetings from Santa 10
    Prancing Toys 14
    Christmas in Toyland 16
    The Nutcracker 18
    Jolly Old St. Nicholas 22
THE DECORATIONS OF CHRISTMAS
    Deck the Hall 23
    Cookies and Cider 24
    Dinner with the March Family 26
    Holly and Mistletoe 30
    The Legend of the Poinsettia 31
THE GIFTS OF CHRISTMAS
    Why We Give Gifts at Christmas 32
    Our Lady's Juggler 34
    We Three Kings 38
    The Twelve Days of Christmas 40
THE TREES OF CHRISTMAS
    The Peterkins' Christmas Tree 42
    Why We Have Christmas Trees 46
    Tree Decorations You Can Make 48
    O Tannenbaum 50
THE ANIMALS OF CHRISTMAS
    The Friendly Beasts 51
    The Innkeeper's Daughter 52
    The Animals' Christmas Tree 56
    Make an Animal Christmas Tree 57
THE SOUNDS OF CHRISTMAS
    A Child's Prayer 58
    I Heard the Bells on Christmas Day 60
    A Christmas Carol 62
    Old Spanish Carol 66
    Angels We Have Heard on High 68
THE BIRTH OF CHRISTMAS
    Christmas Song 70
    The Gospel According to Luke and Matthew 72
    There's a Song in the Air 74
    Away in a Manger 76

ABC's of Christmas

Alice Leedy Mason

A is holy angels
Appearing high above,
Announcing a cappella
God's wondrous gift of love.

B is lowly Bethlehem,
The birthplace of a king,
The Bible with its blessings
And bells that sweetly ring.

C means cards and candles
Are the custom of the day,
While choirs sing Christmas carols
To crowds along the way.

D stands for December,
Decorations to delight,
Dolls and drums and Doberman
Kept secretly from sight.

E says eager shepherds
Went East, led by a star,
As earnest Christians every day
Exalt Him near and far.

F stands for the frankincense
For future times lovefold,
Friendship, family, faithful hearts
And the Father known of old.

G speaks of the gospel,
Good news, the gift of grace,
Of Galilee, the Magi's gold
And great old songs of praise.

H is hearth and holly,
Holidays at home,
Heavenly hosts and humble hearts
And hope for those that roam.

I is for Immanuel
And no room in the inn.
Instead He chose a stable
With peace and love within.

J is Joseph's journey
With Mary long ago,
It's jumping ropes and jerseys
And jewels to wear and show.

K is for kaleidoscopes,
For knitting (almost done),
Kitchens filled with sweets and spice,
And kittens in the sun.

L is for the laughter,
The lavender and lace,
For love that lifts the lonely heart
And lights the stranger's face.

M tells of the manger
And a mother's gentle care,
Mistletoe and miracles
And music everywhere.

N is the Nativity—
That holy night so grand.
It's navy ships and noble thoughts
And neighbors near at hand.

O stands for omnipotent—
One God for you and me.
It's oats to feed the reindeer,
Ornaments on the tree.

P means precious promise.
It's pastry to prepare.
The family plans and presents
Provide for praise and prayer.

Q . . . now that's the question!
Be quick to qualify.
It's quaint old dolls, ducks that quack
And quilts piled shoulder high.

R is for remembrance,
Relatives, rich and poor,
Gifts with bright red ribbons
And recipes galore.

S is for the Savior,
The shepherds and the song,
For sugarplums and sweetmeats
And sleighs that scoot along.

T is for the turkey
With tasty treats to try.
It's toy trains and trees to trim,
Glad tidings from on high.

U might be a unicorn
If unicorns were real.
Instead it's for unusual gifts
That have unique appeal.

V tells of the village
Where the Virgin had her child,
Of vesper bells at evening
And voices sweet and mild.

W stands for wonderful
In the good old-fashioned way,
Christmas wish and Wassail dish
And waiting for the day.

X is toy xylophones
With greetings to express,
Extending hope for health and joy
And extra happiness.

Y is a yellow sports car,
A gourmet Yuletide feast.
It's yachts and yaks and yo-yos
And sweet breads made with yeast.

Z is for old zither tunes,
For zebras at the zoo,
A Christmas blessed with love expressed
From A to Z for YOU!

Greetings from Santa

Author Unknown

He comes in the night! He comes in the night!
He softly, silently comes,
While the little brown heads on the pillows so white
Are dreaming of bugles and drums.
Who tells him, I know not, but he finds the home
Of each good little boy and girl.

His sleigh, it is long and deep and wide;
It will carry a host of things,
While dozens of drums hang over the side,
With the sticks sticking under the strings.
And yet, not the sound of a drum is heard,
Not a bugle blast is blown,
As he mounts to the chimney top like a bird
And drops to the hearth like a stone.

The little red stockings, he silently fills
Till the stockings will hold no more;
The bright little sleds for the great snow hills
Are quickly set down on the floor.
Then Santa Claus mounts to the roof like a bird
And glides to his seat in the sleigh;
Not a sound of a bugle or drum is heard
As he noiselessly gallops away.

He rides to the East, and he rides to the West,
Of his goodies, he touches not one;
He eats the crumbs of the Christmas feast
When the dear little folks are done.
Old Santa Claus does all that he can;
This beautiful mission is his;
Then children, be good to the little old man,
When you find who the little man is.

Prancing Toys

Joan Ashurst

Last night when all the house was still,
I woke up with a start,
To lie with eyes wide open, and
A quickly beating heart.
Then as I listened, all at once
I heard a lot of squeaks,
As if the mice that run around
Had not been fed for weeks.
I tiptoed softly down the stairs
And crept toward the din,
The playroom door stood open, so
I carefully peeped in.
The corner cupboard shook and groaned;
Then to my great surprise,
I saw the handle start to turn
Before my very eyes.
The cupboard door flew open and
Out fell all the toys.
They made more noise than any of
The neighbor's girls and boys.

The policeman marched along in front,
His face all red and jolly,
Then next came by blue teddy bear,
Hand in hand with dolly.
The fairy doll tripped lightly by,
Her wand a sparkling light,
Close on her heels was dolly boy,
His face a winsome sight.
The fluffy rabbit and the dog
Both skipped about with glee,
And everyone was chattering,
A sight it was to see.
The little wooden elephant
Gave Mickey Mouse a ride;
And as he strutted on, he swung
His trunk from side to side.
The soldiers left the castle walls
And joined the merry throng,
The captain led the gay parade
With steps both brisk and long.

The drummer boy a gay tattoo
Did beat upon his drum;
I never heard such merriment
From toys I thought were dumb.
They marched around the room and then
All kinds of games they played,
Like hide-and-seek, and blindman's bluff,
Oh, what a noise they made.
But as the chimes of midnight struck
And slowly died away,
Quite silent they at once became,
No longer bright and gay.
A solemn little band of toys,
They filed across the floor,
Then one by one they climbed inside
And closed the cupboard door.
I waited for a little while,
But it was all in vain;
The spell had broken and they all
Were regular toys again.

Christmas in Toyland

Anton J. Stoffle

The soldiers marched in a gay parade,
Happy the tunes their little band played.
Small plastic dolls with fluttering eyes
Looked at the soldiers with great surprise,
While the china dolls stood on a shelf,
Each one a beauty, proud of herself,

And the other dolls, all dressed in style,
Showed the latest of fashions with a smile.

A jack-in-the-box bounced up and down,
Stealing some laughs from Bobo, the clown.

Lions and tigers, pandas and bears,
Danced about with turtles and hares,
While Cathy, the cat, and Fido, the dog,
Joined in a song with Jumpy, the frog.
Zippo, the monkey, waved a small mop,
And, off in a corner, there spun a top.

King Thor and Queen Anne, on the castle wall,
Were laughing and having themselves a ball,
While the prince and princess danced with the toys.
Fiddlers played on in spite of the noise,

And Santa Claus sat with pipe aglow,
A jolly old gent. How he loved the show!
At Christmas, in Toyland, such scenes you'll view.
Enjoy it, children, it's all for you.

The Nutcracker

Retold by Ronald Kidd

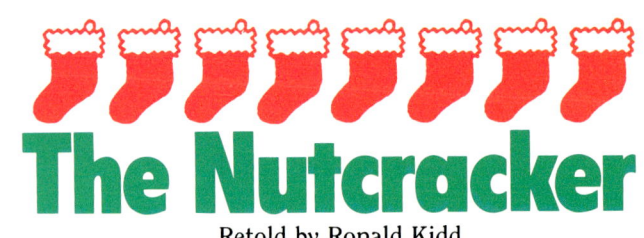

Twelve-year-old Clara Stahlbaum knelt next to a door in the parlor, peeking through the keyhole into the drawing room. Her brother, Fritz, crouched next to her, and behind him stood eight other children.

"What do you see?" said Fritz.

"Nothing yet," she replied. "The grown-ups are just dancing and talking."

A moment later the door swung open and the parlor was flooded with light. Dr. Stahlbaum stood there, beaming. "Merry Christmas, children!" he said.

They raced past him into the drawing room, with Fritz leading the way and Clara following close behind. Before them stood a Christmas tree at least ten feet tall. But it wasn't the tree that caught their attention. It was what lay beneath: presents.

There were sugarplums, bonbons, toy soldiers, miniature swords and cannons, ceramic dolls, silk dresses, wooden horses, picture books, and dozens of other gifts. The children scurried about the tree, discovering treasure after treasure.

Then the front door burst open, and a cold breeze blew through the room. Out of the winter night stepped a man dressed in black. A tall hat covered his head, and he held a cape over his face, hiding everything but his eyes. The guests grew silent. Clara moved to her father's side and took his hand.

The man strode up to the group, the click of his boots echoing off the marble floor. Then he stopped and slowly drew aside the cape.

Behind it was the smiling face of Godpapa Drosselmeier. Besides being Clara's godfather, he was known throughout the village as a fixer of clocks and a master woodcarver and inventor.

"Oh, Godpapa," cried Clara, "you scared us!"

Clara's godfather gave her a big hug. "My dear," he said, "I've brought you and the other children a surprise."

He drew the sides of his cape together in a great circle, and when he opened them, three wooden figures stood on the floor in front of him: a ballerina, a clown, and a Sugar Plum Fairy. The figures began to move.

When the mechanical figures stopped moving, the guests clapped and cheered. Godpapa Drosselmeier took a deep bow, then turned to Clara. "And now," he said, "I have one more surprise. It's a special gift for a very special girl."

"What is it?" asked one of the children looking on.

"It's a nutcracker," replied Clara's godfather.

After the family had gone to bed, Clara lay in her room reliving all that had happened that evening. She gazed at the ceiling, thinking about the tree and the music and most of all the nut-

cracker, whose face was so grotesque and yet somehow so brave. She slipped out of her bed and down the stairs.

The drawing room was dark, but Clara had no trouble picking out the gaily painted face of the nutcracker beneath the Christmas tree. She went over to her new friend, lay down beside him, and fell into a deep sleep.

As the hour approached midnight, there was a noise in the room. Clara awoke and peered into the darkness.

Slinking toward her was a mouse as big as a man. Its eyes were green, and its fur was a dull, matted gray.

Clara rubbed her eyes, then looked again. The mouse was joined by ten others just like it. They circled around her, drawing closer and closer. When they were near enough to touch, the clock chimed the first stroke of midnight.

Next to her, the nutcracker moved. Yawning and stretching, he rose to his feet. Then, as the clock kept striking, he began to grow. By the time the twelfth chime died, he was Nutcracker, a real-life soldier standing six feet tall.

Clara watched as Nutcracker put one arm around her and, with the other, drew his sword. The mice backed away.

There was a puff of smoke and out stepped another mouse. Bigger and uglier than the others, he was the evil Mouse King.

Encouraged by the arrival of their leader, the other mice edged forward once again. Nutcracker brandished his sword, but it was clear that he and Clara would soon be surrounded.

When all seemed lost, a bugle sounded from the direction of the Christmas tree. The toy soldiers were beginning to stir! Clara watched in astonishment as they grew to full size and sprang into action.

Under Nutcracker's orders, they fired their cannon and advanced on the mice. A tremendous struggle followed. First one side, then the other appeared to be winning. The toy soldiers' line heaved forward, and back, and forward again. The room was filled with the sounds of battle.

Nutcracker and the Mouse King crossed swords. The two leaders circled, thrusting and parrying, as Clara shouted encouragement from the side.

Then it happened. The Mouse King lunged and Nutcracker went down. The giant mouse raised its arms in triumph and strutted around its fallen victim.

But Nutcracker struggled to his feet, his face contorted in pain, and challenged the Mouse King once again. The ugly gray creature closed in to finish him off.

Whatever the cause, all Clara saw were the flash of Nutcracker's sword and the sudden halt of his opponent. The Mouse King lay dead on the floor, and Nutcracker had fallen motionless beside him.

The sounds of battle stopped. The mice gathered up the body of their leader and carried it off, their steps slow.

Clara, meanwhile, rushed to the fallen Nutcracker and knelt beside him. She took his hand and smoothed his brow, searching for signs of life. She saw none.

In the silence, there were footsteps. Clara looked up and saw her godfather standing over her.

She threw herself into his arms. "Oh, Godpapa," she cried, "what can I do?"

Her godfather held her close and murmured, "Don't worry, Clara. Godpapa Drosselmeier will fix your dream." He reached down and touched the fallen warrior's shoulder.

Nutcracker's eyes popped open.

Clara gasped, then watched in awe as his face began to change. The bright colors melted together, and the gaping mouth and eyes took on a pleasing shape. Seconds later, Clara was looking at a dashing prince.

"Thank you, Godpapa," she said, hugging the old man tight. "Thank you for saving him."

"Ah, but Clara," he replied, smiling, "it was you who saved him with the power of your love."

Suddenly, Clara was back in the drawing room, alone on the floor beside a small wooden nutcracker. Taking the figure in her arms, she went to the front door and peered out into the night.

Snow was falling in the streets of the village, but Clara didn't see it. She was looking beyond to a land where toy soldiers spring to life and goodness always wins.

Cookies and Cider

Golden Sugar Cookies

- 2½ cups sifted flour
- 1 teaspoon baking soda
- 1 teaspoon cream of tartar
- ¼ teaspoon salt
- 1 cup unsalted butter, softened
- 1 teaspoon vanilla
- ½ teaspoon lemon extract
- 2 cups sugar
- 3 egg yolks

1. Preheat oven to 350°F.
2. Combine flour, soda, cream of tartar, and salt. Set aside.
3. Cream butter, vanilla, and lemon extract until butter is soft and smooth.
4. Gradually add sugar to creamed mixture, beating until fluffy.
5. Add egg yolks, one at a time, beating well after each addition.
6. Add dry ingredients, a little at a time, to the creamed mixture, beating after each addition until blended.
7. Form dough into 1-inch balls. Place about 2 inches apart on ungreased cookie sheet.
8. Bake for 10 minutes or until golden brown.

Christmas Trees

- 2 9½-ounce packages refrigerated cinnamon rolls with icing
- 6 tablespoons granola, raisins, or nuts

1. Preheat oven to 375°F.
2. Cover a 10 x 14-inch baking sheet with foil.
3. Separate rolls. Arrange rolls in rows to simulate a Christmas tree. Starting at the center top of baking sheet, set rolls very closely in rows of 1-2-3-4-5.
4. Bake for 18 to 20 minutes.
5. Remove from oven.
6. While rolls are hot, spread with icing and sprinkle with granola, raisins, or nuts to decorate.

Hot Spiced Cider

- 1 quart apple cider
- 1 2-inch cinnamon stick
- 1 whole nutmeg
- 3 to 4 whole cloves
- 3 to 4 whole allspice
- ½ teaspoon grated orange peel

1. Combine all ingredients in a medium-sized saucepan.
2. Bring to a boil.
3. Turn heat to low and simmer 5 to 15 minutes. (Longer simmering makes a stronger flavor.)
4. Serve in mugs.
5. Decorate with a cinnamon stick in each mug.

Dinner with the March Family

Louisa May Alcott

"Christmas won't be Christmas without any presents," grumbled Jo, lying on the rug.

"It's so dreadful to be poor!" sighed Meg, looking down at her old dress.

"We've got Father and Mother and each other," said Beth contentedly from her corner.

The four young faces on which the firelight shone brightened at the cheerful words.

"The reason Mother proposed not having any presents this Christmas was because it is going to be a hard winter for everyone," Meg said. "She thinks we ought not to spend money for pleasure. We can't do much, but we can make our little sacrifices, and ought to do it gladly."

"Mother didn't say anything about our money, and she won't wish us to give up everything. Let's each buy what we want and have a little fun. I'm sure we work hard enough to earn it," cried Jo.

The clock struck six and, having swept up the hearth, Beth put a pair of slippers down to warm, for Mother was coming, and everyone brightened to welcome her home.

Jo sat up to hold the slippers nearer to the blaze. "They are quite worn out. Marmee must have a new pair."

"I'll tell you what we'll do," said Beth. "Let's each get something for Marmee for Christmas, and not get anything for ourselves."

"That's like you, dear! What will we get?" exclaimed Jo.

Meg announced, "I shall give her a nice pair of gloves."

"Army shoes, the very best to be had," cried Jo.

"Some handkerchiefs, all hemmed," decided Beth with satisfaction.

"I'll get a little bottle of cologne. It won't cost much, so I'll have some left to buy my pencils," added Amy.

"Let Marmee think we are getting things for ourselves, and then surprise her. We must go shopping tomorrow afternoon," said Jo, marching up and down, with her hands behind her back.

Jo was the first to wake in the gray dawn of Christmas morning. She slipped her hand under her pillow and drew out a crimson-covered Bible.

She woke Meg with a "Merry Christmas" and bade her see what was under her pillow—a green-covered Bible. Presently, Beth and Amy woke to rummage and find their little books also—one dove-colored, the other blue.

The rooms were very still while the pages were softly turned, and the winter sunshine crept in to touch the bright heads and serious faces with a Christmas greeting.

"Where is Mother?" asked Meg, as she and Jo ran down to thank her for their gifts, half an hour later.

"Goodness only knows. Some poor creeter come a-beggin', and your ma went straight off to see what was needed," replied Hannah, who had lived with the family since Meg was born and was considered by them all more as a friend than a maid.

"She'll be back soon, I think, so have everything ready," said Meg, looking over the presents which had been collected in a

basket and kept under the sofa, ready to be produced at the proper time.

"There's Mother. Hide the basket, quick!" cried Jo, as the door slammed.

"Merry Christmas, Marmee! Many of them!" they cried in chorus.

"Merry Christmas, little daughters! I want to say one word before we sit down to eat. Not far from here lies a poor woman with a little newborn baby. Six children are huddled into one bed to keep from freezing, for they have no fire. There is nothing to eat over there, and the oldest boy came to tell me they were suffering hunger and cold. My girls, will you give them your Christmas breakfast as a Christmas present?"

For a minute no one spoke—only a minute, for Jo exclaimed impetuously, "I'm so glad you came before we began to eat!"

"May I go and help carry the things to the poor little children?" asked Beth eagerly.

"You shall all go and help me," said Mrs. March, smiling. "And when we come back we will have bread and milk for breakfast and make it up at dinnertime."

They were soon ready, and the procession set out.

A poor, bare, miserable room it was, with broken windows, no fire, ragged bedclothes, a sick mother, a wailing baby, and a group of pale, hungry children cuddled under one old quilt, trying to keep warm.

How the big eyes stared and the blue lips smiled as the girls went in!

"It is good angels come to us!" said the poor woman, crying for joy.

"Funny angels in hoods and mittens," said Jo, and set them laughing.

In a few minutes it really did seem as if kind spirits had been at work there. Hannah, who had carried wood, made a fire and stopped up the broken panes with old hats and her own cloak. Mrs. March gave the mother tea and gruel and comforted her with promises of help, while she dressed the little baby as tenderly as if it had been her own. The girls, meantime, spread the table, set the children round the fire, and fed them like so many hungry birds—laughing and talking.

That was a very happy breakfast, though they didn't get any of it. When they went away, leaving comfort behind, I think there were not in all the city four merrier people than the hungry little girls who gave away

their breakfasts and contented themselves with bread and milk on Christmas morning.

"That's loving our neighbor better than ourselves, and I like it," said Meg, as they set out their presents while their mother was upstairs.

"She's coming! Strike up, Beth! Open the door, Amy! Three cheers for Marmee!" cried Jo, prancing about while Meg went to conduct Mother to the seat of honor.

Mrs. March was both surprised and touched as she examined her presents and the little notes which accompanied them. The slippers went on at once, a new handkerchief was slipped into her pocket, well scented with Amy's cologne, a rose from Beth was fastened in her belt, and the gloves were pronounced "a perfect fit."

A few happy hours later, Hannah appeared, with Mrs. March's compliments, and would the ladies walk down to supper.

When the girls saw the table, they looked at one another in rapturous amazement. There was ice cream—actually two dishes of it, pink and white—and cake and fruit and distracting French bonbons and, in the middle of the table, four great bouquets of hothouse flowers!

"Is it fairies?" asked Amy.

"It's Santa Claus," said Beth.

"Mother did it," said Meg.

"All wrong. Old Mr. Laurence sent it," replied Mrs. March.

"The Laurence boy's grandfather! What in the world put such a thing into his head?" exclaimed Meg.

Hannah told one of his servants about your breakfast party, and that pleased him. He sent me a polite note saying he hoped I would allow him to express his friendly feeling toward my children by sending them a few trifles in honor of the day. I could not refuse, and so you have a little feast to make up for the bread-and-milk breakfast."

"What a special Christmas this has turned out to be!" exclaimed Meg, smelling her flowers.

"Merry Christmas, girls," said Mrs. March, with her arms open wide to embrace her little women.

"Merry Christmas, Marmee!" they cried in unison.

Holly and Mistletoe

Pamela Kennedy

Along with the fir tree, other green plants are honored at Christmas. Holly, with its dark green leaves and bright red berries, reflects the colors of Christmas on each branch. Long ago, children searched the woods for branches of holly to decorate their homes. Many believed that decking the halls with boughs of holly brought good cheer and health to the family throughout the year.

Mistletoe, too, was gathered and brought home. The small white berries were thought to bring good luck and love. For this reason, people fastened sprigs of mistletoe above each doorway in their homes. When a girl passed beneath the mistletoe, a young man could give her a kiss—but only if he gave her a berry from the mistletoe. When the berries were gone, so were the kisses!

This Christmas, if you have mistletoe in your home, you might like to play a game that was played by children over 300 years ago in England. Join hands with your friends and form a circle under the hanging mistletoe. Choose one person to toss a shoe into the center of the circle. He tries to get the shoe to land under the mistletoe. If he fails, he passes the shoe to the person next to him. When the shoe lands under the mistletoe, the one tossing it runs to catch the person to whom the shoe points. That person tries to grab the shoe before being caught. If he is tagged, it becomes his turn to toss the shoe.

The Legend of the Poinsettia

Pamela Kennedy

Aleta stood beside the dusty road watching her friends and neighbors hurry past. It was a warm December night in the little Mexican village, and the ringing of church bells filled the air.

"Come on, Aleta!" shouted her friends. "Hurry! You'll be late!"

But Aleta only shook her head and turned away. Her eyes filled with tears.

It was the most holy night of the year, Christmas Eve. It seemed that everyone was filled with joy as they hurried to the church, carrying armfuls of beautiful flowers to place around the manger scene. The flowers were gifts for the Christ Child and his mother, Mary.

But Aleta had nothing to bring. No flowers bloomed beside her tiny home, and there was no money to buy them from the flower seller. As Aleta turned to walk away, an angel suddenly appeared beside her.

"Why are you so sad, child?" the angel asked.

Through her tears, Aleta told the angel she had nothing to bring the Christ Child this holy night.

"But you do, my dear. You have your love. And that can make the simplest gift a wonderful treasure. Cut these roadside weeds and carry them to the church. There you will see the miracle of love."

Afraid, but wanting to obey the angel, Aleta did as she was told. Slowly, with downcast eyes, she walked through the crowded church carrying her bundle of dusty weeds.

As she placed them before the manger scene, Aleta bowed her head in prayer. Suddenly a strange and wonderful thing happened. The ugly weeds became the blooms we now know as the poinsettia.

Ever since that night, the poinsettia has been known as the Christmas flower, and its scarlet blossoms are a reminder of the miracle of Christmas love.

Why We Give Gifts at Christmas

Pamela Kennedy

Of all the Christmas customs, the giving and receiving of gifts seems to be the favorite of children everywhere. It is thought that this custom began as a way of remembering the wonderful gifts brought to the Christ by the Magi. Some feel, however, that our gifts recall the gift God gave to humankind in sending His Son as Savior.

Whatever the beginning of the tradition, gift giving seems to take place all over the world at Christmastime. But as with other customs, gift giving is done differently in different places.

In the United States, Santa Claus brings gifts to children on Christmas Eve or Christmas morning and leaves them in stockings or under the tree. In Germany, however, it is a messenger from the Christ Child, or Kris Kringle, who brings the gifts. He is usually dressed in robes, wearing a golden crown and carrying a small Christmas tree.

In Czechoslovakia an angel travels with St. Nicholas and bestows the gifts. In Switzerland, St. Lucy helps Father Christmas deliver presents to the good children.

Perhaps Syria has the most unusual Christmas messenger. There it is an animal who brings Christmas gifts. The Camel of Jesus, said to be the youngest camel who traveled with the Wise Men, bears Christmas presents to Syrian children.

In other countries, such as Holland and Belgium, gifts are given not on Christmas Day, but on December 6, called St. Nicholas's Day. And in Poland, Spain, Italy, and Russia gifts are often given on the Twelfth Night, or January 6, to remember the coming of the Wise Men several days after Jesus' birth.

American children are accustomed to finding gifts in stockings or under the Christmas tree, but many other children find them elsewhere. In some European countries, gifts are placed in shoes, and in many South American countries children find their Christmas gifts in a cradle or crib. This is to remind them of the manger where the Baby Jesus was placed.

Whatever the way and whatever the day, the giving of gifts at Christmastime is one way we share love with our families and friends.

Our Lady's Juggler

Anatole France

In the days when the world was young, there lived in France a man of no importance. Everyone said he was a man of no importance, and he firmly believed this himself. For he was just a poor traveling juggler, who could not read or write, who went about from town to town following the little country fairs and performing his tricks for a few pennies a day. His name was Barnaby.

When the weather was beautiful, and people were strolling about the streets, this juggler would find a clear space in the Village Square, spread a strip of old carpet out on the cobblestones, and on it he would perform his tricks for children and grown-ups alike. Now Barnaby, although he knew he was a man of no importance, was an amazing juggler.

First he would only balance a tin plate on the tip of his nose. But when the crowd had collected, he would stand on his hands and juggle six copper balls in the air at the same time, catching them with his feet. And sometimes, when he would juggle twelve sharp knives in the air, the villagers would be so delighted that a rain of pennies would fall on his strip of carpet. And when his day's work was over, and he was wearily resting his aching muscles, Barnaby would collect the pennies in his hat, kneel down reverently, and thank God for the gift.

Always the people would laugh at his simplicity and everyone would agree that Barnaby would never amount to anything. But all this is about the happy days in Barnaby's life, the springtime days when people were willing to toss a penny to a poor juggler. When winter came, Barnaby had to wrap his juggling equipment in the carpet, and trudge along the roads begging a night's lodging in farmers' barns, or entertaining the servants of some rich nobleman to earn a meal. And Barnaby never thought of complaining—he knew that the winter and the rains were as necessary as the spring sunshine, and he accepted his lot. "For how," Barnaby would say to himself as he trudged along, "could such an ignorant fellow as myself hope for anything better."

And one year in France there was a terrible winter. It began to rain in October, and there was hardly a blue sky to be seen by the end of November. And on an evening in early December at the end of a dreary, wet day, as Barnaby trudged along a country road, sad and bent, carrying under his arm the golden balls and knives wrapped up in his old carpet, he met a monk. Riding a fine white mule, dressed in warm clothes, well fed and comfortable, the monk smiled at the sight of Barnaby and called to him: "It's going to be cold before morning. How would you like to spend the night at the monastery?"

And that night Barnaby found himself seated in the great candlelit dining hall of the monastery. Although he sat at the bottom of the long table, together

with the servants and beggars, Barnaby thought he had never seen such a wonderful sight in his life—the shining faces of fifty monks relaxing after this day of work and prayer.

Barnaby did not dare to suggest that he should perform his tricks, as they would be sacrilege before such men; but as he ate and drank more than he had ever had at a meal for years, a great resolution came over him. Although it made him tremble at his own boldness, as the meal ended, Barnaby suddenly arose, ran around the table down to where the lordly abbot sat at the head, and sank to his knees. "Father, grant my prayer! Let me stay in this wonderful place and work for you! I cannot hope to become one of you, I am too ignorant; but let me work in the kitchen and the fields and worship with you in the chapel!"

The monk who had met Barnaby on the road turned to the abbot: "This is a good man, simple and pure of heart." So the abbot nodded, and Barnaby that night put his juggling equipment under a cot in his own cubicle, and decided that never again would he go back to his old profession.

And in the days that followed, everyone smiled at the eager way he scrubbed the floors and labored throughout the buildings; and everyone smiled at his simplicity. As for Barnaby, his face shone with happiness from morning until night.

Until two weeks before Christmas—then Barnaby's joy suddenly turned to misery. For around him he saw every man preparing a wonderful gift to place in the chapel on Christmas—Brother Maurice, who had the art of illuminating copies of the Bible, and Brother Marbode, who was completing a marvelous statue of Christ. Brother Ambrose, who wrote music, had completed the scoring of a great hymn to be played on the organ during Christmas services.

All about Barnaby those educated, trained artists followed their work, each one of them readying a beautiful gift to dedicate to God on Christmas Day. And what about Barnaby? He could do nothing. "I am but a rough man, unskilled in the arts, and I can write no book, offer no painting or statue or poem. Alas, I have no talent, I have no gift worthy of the day!"

So Barnaby sank deep into sadness and despair. Christmas Day came, and the chapel was resplendent with the gifts of the brothers. The giant organ rang with the new music; the choir sang the chorales; the candles glittered around the great new statue. And Barnaby was not there. He was in his tiny cubicle, praying forgiveness for having no gift to offer.

Then a strange thing happened. On the evening of Christmas Day, when the chapel should have been deserted, one of the monks came running, white-faced and panting with exertion, into the private office of the abbot. He threw open the door without knocking, and seized the abbot by the arms. "Father, a frightful thing is happening. The most terrible sacrilege ever to take place is going on right in our own chapel! Come!"

Together the two portly men ran down the corridors, burst through a door, and came out on the balcony at the rear of the chapel. The monk pointed down toward the altar. The abbot looked and turned ashen in color. "He is mad!"

For down below, in front of the altar, was Barnaby. He had spread out his strip of carpet and, kneeling reverently upon it, was actually juggling in the air twelve golden balls! He was giving his old performance, and giving it beautifully—his bright knives, the shining balls, the tin plate balanced on the tip of his nose. And on his face was a look of adoration and joy.

"We must seize him at once," cried the abbot, and turned for the door. But at that moment a light filled the church, a brilliant beam of light coming directly from the altar. Both monks sank to their knees.

For as Barnaby knelt exhausted on his carpet, they saw the statue of the Virgin Mary move. She stepped down from her pedestal, and coming to where Barnaby knelt, took the blue hem of her robe and touched it to his forehead, gently drying the perspiration that glistened there. Then the light dimmed. Up in the choir balcony the monk looked at his superior: "God accepted the only gift he had to make."

And the abbot slowly nodded: "Blessed are the simple in heart . . . for they shall see God."

We Three Kings

We three Kings of Orient are,
   Bearing gifts we traverse afar,
Field and fountain, moor and mountain,
   Following yonder star.

CHORUS:
O, star of wonder,
Star of night,
Star with royal beauty bright,
Westward leading, still proceeding,
Guide us to Thy perfect light.

Gaspar:
Born a King on Bethlehem plain,
   Gold I bring, to crown Him again,
King forever, ceasing never,
   Over us all to reign.
CHORUS

Melchior:
Frankincense to offer have I;
   Incense owns a Deity nigh:
Prayer and praising, all men raising,
   Worship Him, God on high.
CHORUS

Balthasar:
Myrrh is mine; its bitter perfume
   Breathes a life of gathering gloom;
Sorrowing, sighing, bleeding, dying,
   Sealed in the stone-cold tomb.
CHORUS

Glorious now behold Him arise,
   King, and God, and sacrifice,
Heav'n sings alleluia:
   Alleluia the earth replies.
CHORUS

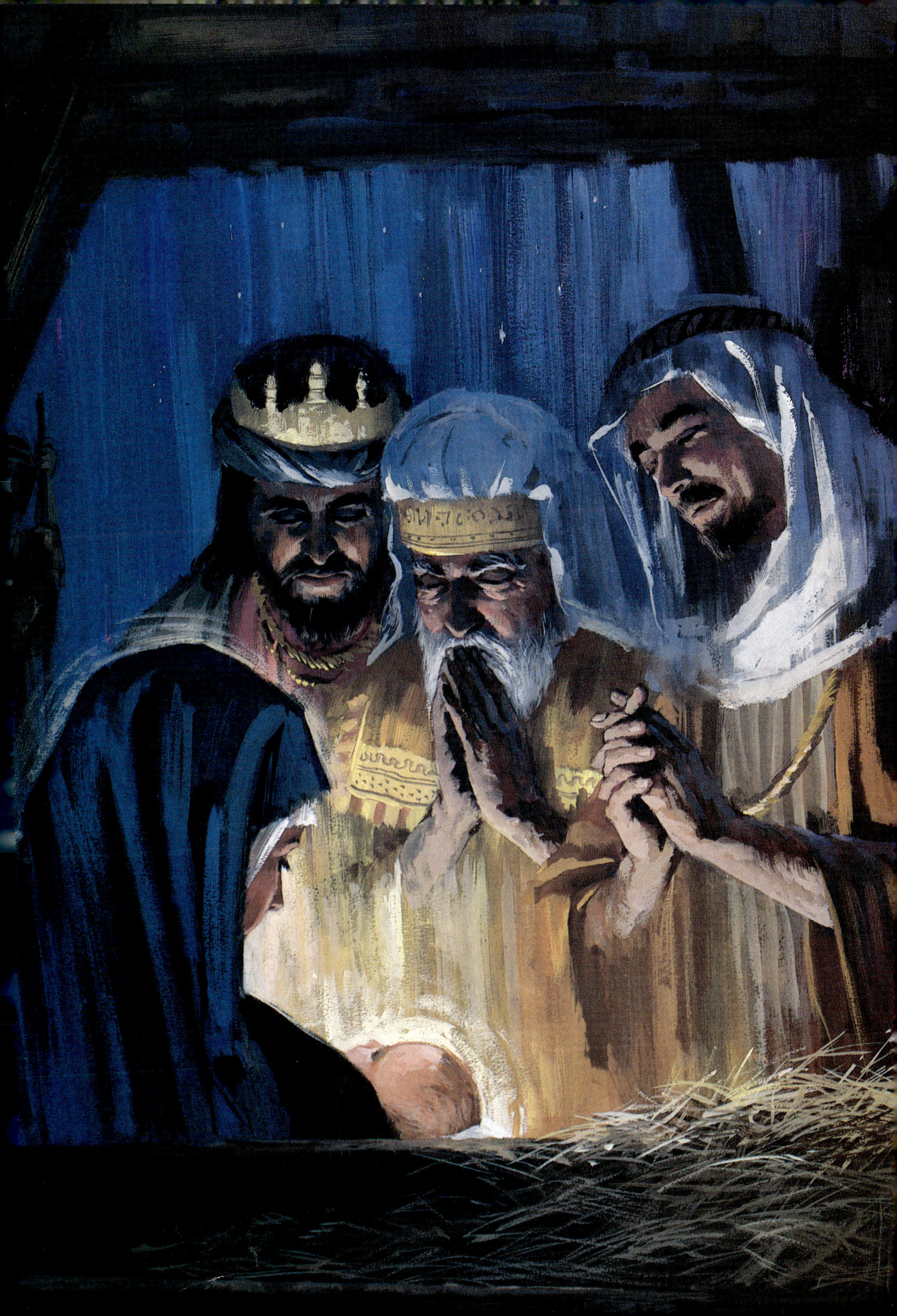

The Twelve Days of Christmas

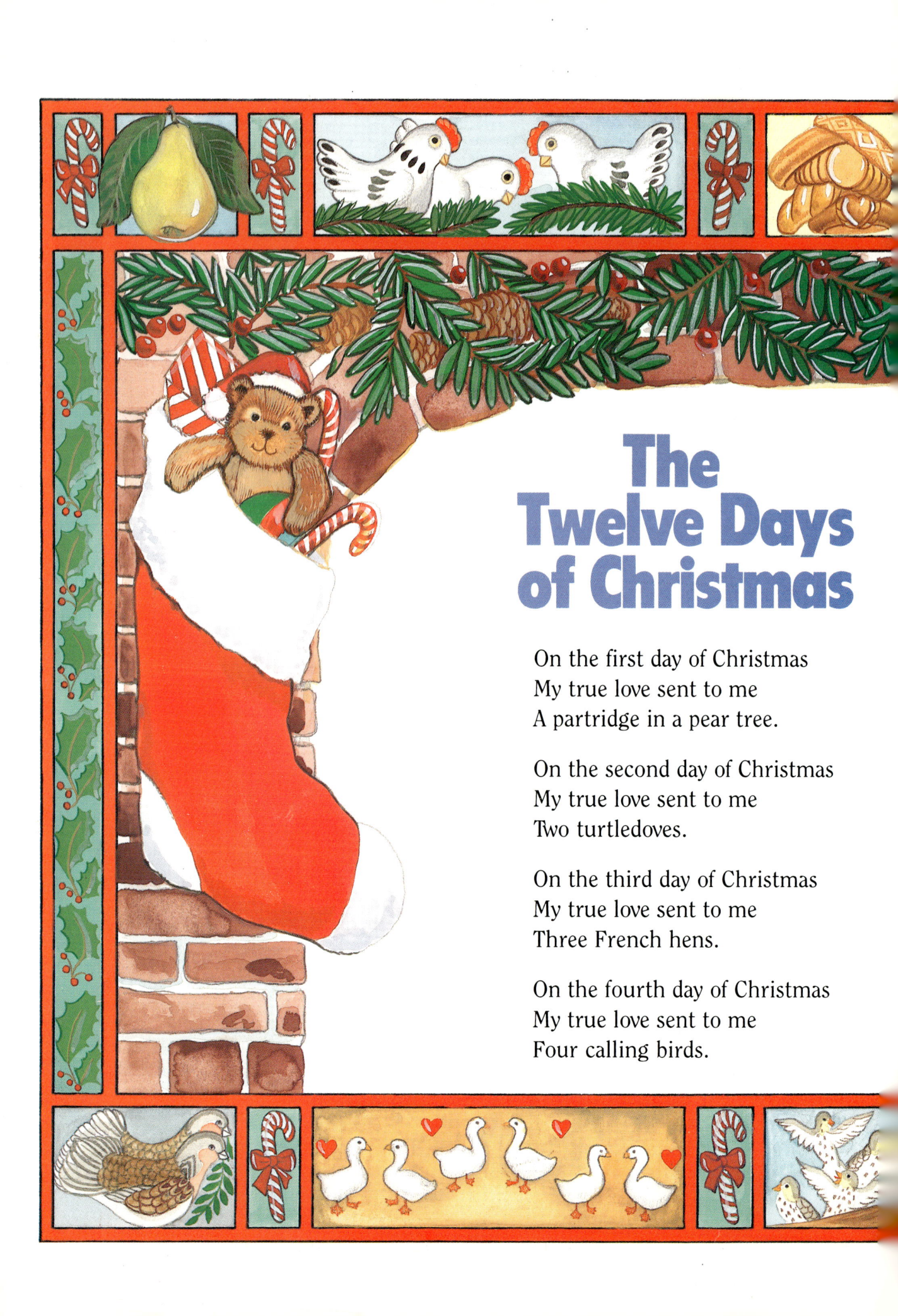

On the first day of Christmas
My true love sent to me
A partridge in a pear tree.

On the second day of Christmas
My true love sent to me
Two turtledoves.

On the third day of Christmas
My true love sent to me
Three French hens.

On the fourth day of Christmas
My true love sent to me
Four calling birds.

On the fifth day of Christmas
My true love sent to me
Five gold rings.

On the sixth day of Christmas
My true love sent to me
Six geese a-laying.

On the seventh day of Christmas
My true love sent to me
Seven swans a-swimming.

On the eighth day of Christmas
My true love sent to me
Eight maids a-milking.

On the ninth day of Christmas
My true love sent to me
Nine ladies dancing.

On the tenth day of Christmas
My true love sent to me
Ten lords a-leaping.

On the eleventh day of Christmas
My true love sent to me
Eleven pipers piping.

On the twelfth day of Christmas
My true love sent to me
Twelve drummers drumming,
Eleven pipers piping,
Ten lords a-leaping,
Nine ladies dancing,
Eight maids a-milking,
Seven swans a-swimming,
Six geese a-laying,
Five gold rings . . .
Four calling birds,
Three French hens,
Two turtledoves
And a partridge in a pear tree.

The Peterkins' Christmas Tree

Lucretia P. Hale

Pretty early in the autumn the Peterkins began to prepare for their Christmas tree. Everything was done in great privacy, as it was to be a surprise to the neighbors, as well as to the rest of the family. Mr. Peterkin had been up to Mr. Bromwich's woodlot, and, with his consent, selected the tree. Agamemnon went to look at it occasionally after dark, and Solomon John made frequent visits to it, mornings, just after sunrise. Mr. Peterkin drove Elizabeth Eliza and her mother that way and pointed furtively to it with his whip, but none of them ever spoke of it aloud to each other. It was suspected that the little boys had been to see it Wednesday and Saturday afternoons. But they came home with their pockets full of chestnuts and said nothing about it.

At length Mr. Peterkin had it cut down and brought secretly into the Larkins' barn. A week or two before Christmas, a measurement was made of it with Elizabeth Eliza's yard measure. To Mr. Peterkin's great dismay, it was discovered that it was too high to stand in the back parlor. This fact was brought out at a secret council of Mr. and Mrs. Peterkin, Elizabeth Eliza, and Agamemnon.

Agamemnon suggested that it might be set up slanting, but Mrs. Peterkin was very sure it would make her dizzy, and the candles would drip.

But a brilliant idea came to Mr. Peterkin. He proposed that the ceiling of the parlor should be raised to make room for the top of the tree.

Elizabeth Eliza thought the space would need to be quite large. It must not be like a small box, or you could not see the tree.

"Yes," said Mr. Peterkin, "I should have the ceiling lifted all across the room; the effect would be finer."

Elizabeth Eliza objected to having the whole ceiling raised, because her room was over the back parlor, and she would have no floor while the alteration was going on, which would be very awkward. Besides, her room was not very high now, and if the floor were raised, perhaps she could not walk in it upright.

Mr. Peterkin explained that he didn't propose altering the whole ceiling, but to lift up a ridge across the room at the back part where the tree was to stand. This would make a hump, to be sure, in Elizabeth Eliza's room, but it would go across the whole room.

Elizabeth Eliza said she would not mind that. It would be like the cuddy thing that comes up on the deck of a ship, that you sit against, only here you would not have the seasickness. She thought she should like it for a rarity. She might use it for a divan.

Mrs. Peterkin thought it would come in the worn place in the carpet, and might be a convenience in making the carpet over.

Agamemnon was afraid there would be trouble in keeping the matter secret, for it would be a long piece of work for a carpenter; but Mr. Peterkin proposed having the carpenter for a day or two, for a number of other jobs.

The carpenter, however, insisted that the tree could be cut off at the lower end to suit the height of the parlor and demurred at so great a change as altering the ceiling. But Mr. Peterkin had set his mind upon the improvement, and Elizabeth Eliza had cut her carpet in preparation for it.

So the folding doors into the back parlor were closed, and for nearly a fortnight before Christmas there was a great litter of fallen plastering, and laths, and chips, and shavings; and Elizabeth Eliza's carpet was taken up, and the furniture had to be changed, and one night she had to sleep at the Bromwiches', for there was a long hole in her floor that might be dangerous.

All this delighted the little boys. They could not understand what was going on. Perhaps they suspected a Christmas tree, but they did not know why a Christmas tree should have so many chips, and were still more astonished at the hump that appeared in Elizabeth Eliza's room. It must be a Christmas present, or else the tree in a box.

Some aunts and uncles, too, arrived a day or two before Christmas with some small cousins. These cousins occupied the attention of the little boys, and there was a great deal of whispering and mystery behind doors, and under the stairs, and in the corners of the entry.

Solomon John was busy, privately making some candles for the tree. He had been collecting some bayberries, as he understood they made very nice candles, so that it would not be necessary to buy any.

The elders of the family never all went into the back parlor together, and all tried not to see what was going on. Mrs. Peterkin would go in with Solomon John, or Mr. Peterkin would go with Elizabeth Eliza, or Elizabeth Eliza would go with Agamemnon and Solomon John. The little boys and the small cousins were never allowed even to look inside the room.

Elizabeth Eliza, meanwhile, went into town a number of times. She wanted to consult Amanda as to how much ice cream they should need, and whether they could make it at home, as they had cream and ice. She was pretty busy in her own room; the furniture had to be changed, and the carpet altered. The "hump" was higher than she had expected. There was danger of bumping her own head whenever she crossed it. She had to nail some padding on the ceiling for fear of accidents.

The afternoon before Christmas, Elizabeth Eliza, Solomon John, and their father collected in the back parlor for a council. The carpenters had done their work, and the tree stood at its full height at the back of the room, the top stretching up into the space arranged for it. All the chips and shavings were cleared away, and it stood on a neat box.

But what were they to put upon the tree?

Solomon John had brought in his supply of candles, but they proved to be very "stringy" and very few. It was strange how many bayberries it took to make a few candles! The little boys had helped him, and he had gathered as much as a bushel of bayberries. He had put them in water and skimmed off the wax, according to the directions, but there was so little wax!

After all her trips into town, Elizabeth Eliza had forgotten to bring anything for the tree.

"I thought of candies and sugar-plums," she said, "but I concluded if we made caramels ourselves we should not need them. But, then, we have not made caramels. The fact is, that day my head was full of my carpet. I had bumped it pretty badly, too.

"It is odd I should have forgotten, that day I went in on purpose to get the things," said Elizabeth Eliza, musingly. "But I went from shop to shop and didn't know exactly what to get. I saw a great many gilt things for Christmas trees, but I knew the little boys were making the gilt apples; there were plenty of candles in the shops, but I knew Solomon John was making the candles."

Mr. Peterkin thought it was quite natural.

Solomon John wondered if it were too late for them to go into town now.

Elizabeth Eliza could not go the next morning, for there was to be a grand Christmas dinner, and Mr. Peterkin could not be spared, and Solomon John was sure he and Agamemnon would not know what to buy. Besides, they would want to try the candles tonight.

A gloom came over the room. There was only a flickering gleam from one of Solomon John's candles that he had lighted by way of trial.

Solomon John again proposed going into town. He lighted a match to read in the newspaper about the trains. There were plenty of trains coming out of town at that hour, but none going in except a very late one. That would not leave time to do anything and come back.

Agamemnon was summoned in. Mrs. Peterkin was entertaining the uncles and aunts in the front parlor. Agamemnon wished there were time to study up on electric lights. Solomon John's candle sputtered and went out.

At this moment there was a loud knocking at the front door. The little boys, and the small cousins, and the uncles and aunts, and Mrs. Peterkin hastened to see what was the matter.

The uncles and aunts thought somebody's house must be on fire. The door was opened and there was a man, white with flakes, for it was beginning to snow, and he was pulling in a large box.

Mrs. Peterkin supposed it contained some of Elizabeth Eliza's purchases, so she ordered it to be pushed into the back parlor, and hastily called back her guests and the boys into the other room. The little boys and the small cousins were sure they had seen Santa Claus himself.

Mr. Peterkin lighted the gas. The box was addressed to Elizabeth Eliza. It was from the lady from Philadelphia! She had gathered a hint from Elizabeth Eliza's letters that there was to be a Christmas tree, and she had filled this box with all that would be needed.

It was opened directly. There was every kind of gilt hanging thing, from gilt pods to butterflies on springs. There were shining flags and lanterns, and birdcages, and nests with birds sitting on them, baskets of fruit, gilt apples and bunches of grapes, and, at the bottom of the whole, a large box of candles and a box of Philadelphia bonbons!

Elizabeth Eliza and Solomon John could scarcely keep from screaming. The little boys and the small cousins knocked on the folding doors to ask what was the matter.

Hastily Mr. Peterkin and the rest took out the things and hung them on the tree and put on the candles.

When all was done, it looked so well that Mr. Peterkin exclaimed:

"Let us light the candles now, and send to invite all the neighbors tonight, and have the tree on Christmas Eve!"

And so it was that the Peterkins had their Christmas tree the day before, and on Christmas night could go and visit their neighbors.

Why We Have Christmas Trees

Pamela Kennedy

Does it seem strange to you that once a year we bring a tree inside the house, then decorate it with ornaments and sparkling lights? Perhaps you have wondered how this custom began.

Many hundreds of years ago, it is said, St. Boniface traveled from England to Germany to tell the people about the Christ Child. At that time, the people in Germany worshipped pagan gods around a huge oak tree. To stop this, St. Boniface cut down the sacred tree, but when he did, a strange thing happened. The oak split into four parts, and a small green fir tree sprang up in its place. St. Boniface told the people that this evergreen tree pointed to the heavens to remind them of the Christ Child born at Christmastime. Whenever they looked upon the lovely green tree they were to think of God's love and kindness. From then on, people in Germany cut small evergreen trees each year at Christmas and placed them in their homes.

At first, these trees were not decorated, but there is another legend explaining how we came to place lights upon our Christmas trees. It is said that Martin Luther, a church reformer, was walking in the woods one clear night in December. Stopping to gaze at the starry skies, he thought that the first Christmas night must have been just as beautiful, with stars twinkling in the dark sky. In order to share this idea with his small son, Luther cut down a little fir tree and took it home. Once inside, he placed the tree on a table and decorated its branches with small candles. The twinkling candlelight against the dark green fir needles looked like the stars in the Christmas sky.

Now we place many colored lights and ornaments on our trees, but the Christmas tree is still a reminder of that very first Christmas long ago. And the joy and beauty it brings to our homes and hearts are a special gift of the Christmas season.

47

Tree Decorations You Can Make

Pamela Kennedy

Many children love to make their own decorations to place upon their Christmas trees. Perhaps this year you would like to try some of the ideas listed below. Because Christmas is a holiday celebrated around the world, we thought you might like to make some decorations to remind you of foreign countries.

JAPAN. The paper fan is a lovely reminder of this oriental country. Cut small rectangles of foil wrapping paper, then fold the rectangles in an accordian fashion. Tie a piece of thread or fine string near one end of the folded paper and fan out the folds above the string to make a Japanese fan to place on your tree.

CZECHOSLOVAKIA. Eggs are a favorite Christmas decoration in this European country. Save eggshell halves, and wash and dry them carefully. From old Christmas cards or magazines, cut small Christmas pictures or designs. Soak them in water to make them shape easily. Glue the paper picture inside the eggshell half, and place a bit of glue around the broken edge of the shell. Dip the shell edge in glitter. When dry, hang your special ornaments from the branches of your tree.

DENMARK. Wooden ornaments are a favorite in Denmark. To make a simple wooden ornament, glue several flat toothpicks in a star design, placing a drop of glue in the center to hold the picks together. By crisscrossing three or four toothpicks you can make a delightful Christmas star to hang on your tree.

ENGLAND. Children in England love to hang candy on their Christmas trees. You can make pretend candy canes by twisting together one white and one red pipe cleaner. After you have twisted them, bend over one end to form the hook on the cane, and hang your English ornament upon your tree.

RUSSIA. Beautiful fabric ornaments are a favorite in Russia. You can make your own fabric ornaments by gluing scraps of pretty fabric onto small styrofoam balls. Overlap the fabric so the ball does not show through. Pin a ribbon loop into the top of each ball for hanging.

SWEDEN. In the north countries like Sweden, snow is usually on the ground at Christmas. Perhaps it is for this reason that the snowflake is a favorite Christmas decoration. To make your own snowflakes, fold squares of white tissue paper into triangles several times, then cut out bits of paper. Unfold your squares to see the lovely flakes you have designed. These may be placed on the boughs of your tree to remind you of winter snow.

YUGOSLAVIA. In Yugoslavia the people love to decorate their trees with paper chains and garlands. Tape or glue strips of colored paper into loops, and hook together to form chains.

UNITED STATES. Stringing popcorn and cranberries to decorate the Christmas tree is an old American custom. Remember to let your popcorn sit for a day so it will string well without crumbling, then use a needle threaded with dental floss or kite string to string your berries and popcorn. You might also try stringing gumdrops or pasta.

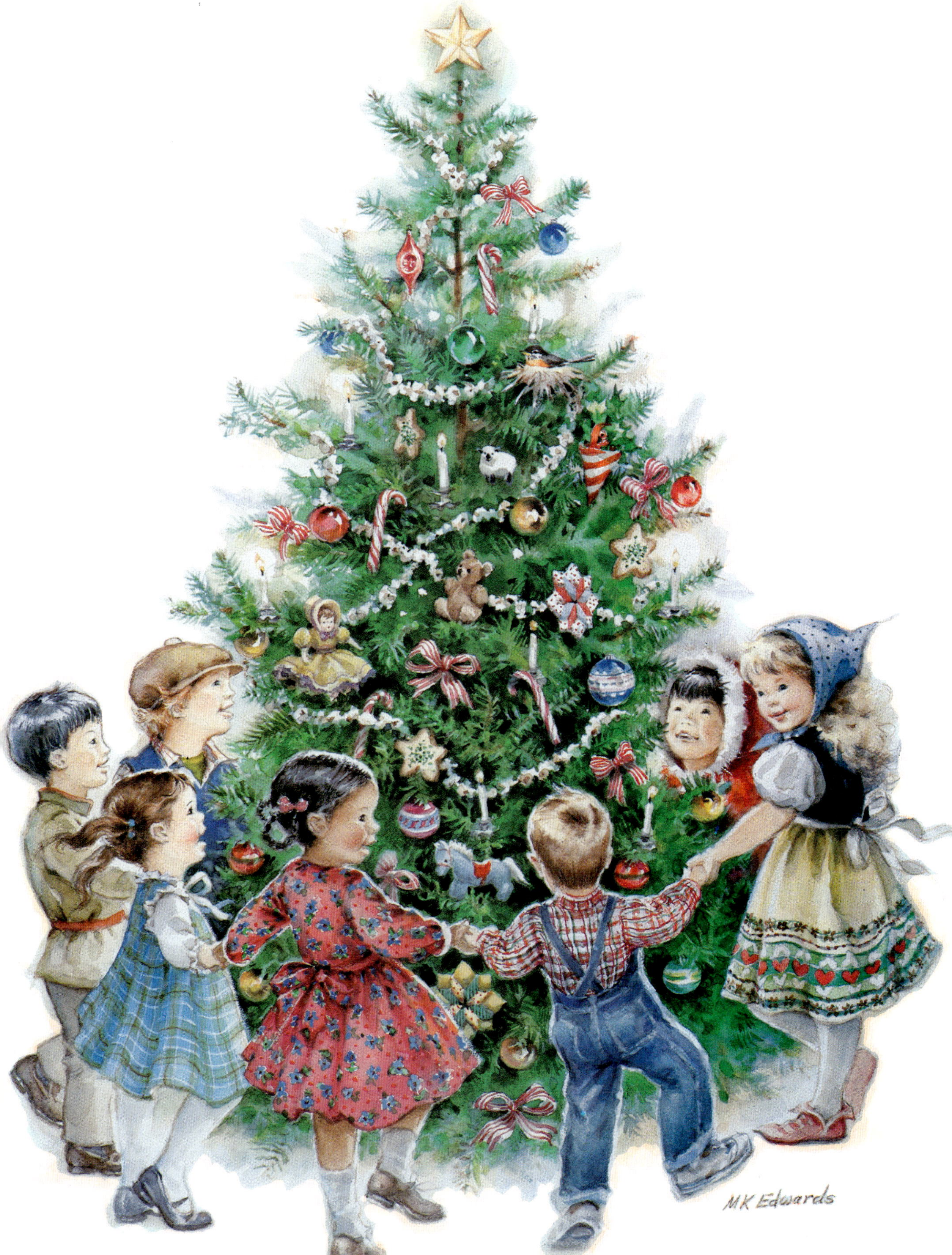
M K Edwards

O Christmas Tree

O Tannenbaum

Translated from the German
English version by RUTH HELLER

GERMAN

Happily

1. O Christ-mas tree, O Christ-mas tree, O tree of green, un-chang-ing. Your boughs, so green in sum-mer time, Do brave the snow of win-ter-time. O Christ-mas tree, O Christ-mas tree, O tree of green, un-chang-ing.
2. O Christ-mas tree, O Christ-mas tree, You set my heart a-sing-ing. Like lit-tle stars, your can-dles bright Send to the world a won-drous light. O Christ-mas tree, O Christ-mas tree, You set my heart a-sing-ing.
3. O Christ-mas tree, O Christ-mas tree, You come from God, e-ter-nal. A sym-bol of the Lord of Love Whom God to man sent from a-bove. O Christ-mas tree, O Christ-mas tree, You come from God, e-ter-nal.
4. O Christ-mas tree, O Christ-mas tree, You speak of God, un-chang-ing. You tell us all to faith-ful be, And trust in God e-ter-nal-ly. O Christ-mas tree, O Christ-mas tree, You speak of God, un-chang-ing.

The Friendly Beasts

Robert Davis

12th Century English
arr. Leland B. Sateren, 1954

Andantino

1. Jesus, our brother, kind and good, Was humbly born in a stable rude, And the friendly beasts around him stood; Jesus, our brother, kind and good.
2. "I", said the cow, all white and red, "I gave him my manger for his bed, I gave him my hay to pillow his head, I", said the cow, all white and red.
3. "I", said the dove from the rafters high, "Cooed him to sleep that he should not cry, We cooed him to sleep my mate and I, I", said the dove from the rafters high.

"I", said the donkey, shaggy and brown, "I carried his mother up hill and down; I carried his mother to Bethlehem town. I", said the donkey shaggy and brown.

"I", said the sheep with curly horn, "I gave him my wool for his blanket warm, He wore my coat on Christmas morn. I", said the sheep with curly horn.

Thus ev'ry beast by some good spell, In the stable dark was glad to tell Of the gift he gave Emmanuel. The gift he gave Emmanuel.

The Innkeeper's Daughter

Jill Briscoe

Keturah was unhappy, so she ran to the stable where she usually went when things went wrong. She loved the animals who were kept there, especially Donkey. He was her favorite. He was gentle and sweet and rubbed his soft nose in her hair when she was upset. She always felt better when she'd had a talk with Donkey.

Keturah had needed a place to run to ever since she discovered she was different from other children. Keturah had crippled hands. She felt awful when a ball was thrown to her and she couldn't catch it or when a kitten needed petting and she couldn't pick it up.

Keturah found her way to the darkest corner of the stable where Donkey was kept. She sat quietly, brushing the animal's side with her nose, wishing she could tickle him with her fingers. One of his hooves was bent. She knew he understood just how she felt. She wondered why God had given fingers to all of her friends but had not given them to her. She knew it could not have been because she was naughty, because God didn't punish people like that. It wouldn't be right and God always did what was right. Keturah sighed and tried not to think about it anymore.

The stable was more crowded than usual. Keturah's father had told her that the Romans, who ruled her town of Bethlehem, had ordered everyone to return to the city of his birth so they could take a census. The visitors kept coming, and soon the stable could not hold any more animals.

That night Keturah had the strangest dream; at least she thought it was a dream. She saw a blinding light coming from a slit in the roof. Looking through the slit she saw the most beautiful star she had ever seen. It was all the colors of a rainbow. She had never seen a star so bright or with such an odd shape. It had one long finger that was pointing right down to the stable!

Suddenly the bright light made the stable look as bright as day, and Keturah could not believe what she was seeing.

The stable was full of children. Where have they all come from, Keturah wondered. She didn't recognize one of them and was quite sure they didn't live in the village. They were small and chubby and had wings!

One of the chubby cherubs (for that was indeed what they were) was trying to comb the dust out of Donkey's tail. The small angel had a dirty face and a black stain right down his beautiful, white clothes.

"Oh dear," he puffed. "I'm not used to doing this. We don't have donkeys at home!"

"Where's home?" asked Keturah shyly, but the cherub didn't answer, even though he glanced at her with a mischievous twinkle.

Donkey loved it! Peeping around Donkey's stall, Keturah saw that all the other animals had been groomed as well.

"They're coming soon," one of the cherubs whispered in Donkey's ear. He seemed to understand and shuffled his hooves excitedly as if he were doing a little dance.

"Who's coming soon?" Keturah asked Donkey, overhearing the words. But Donkey didn't answer.

Suddenly there was a commotion at the stable door. Three huge camels loomed in the opening. Keturah had never seen camels at such close quarters before.

"I hope they're not going to try to come in here as well," Keturah whispered to Donkey. But the camels were tied up in the courtyard and left there. Looking around the stable, Keturah was shocked to find the cherubs had all disappeared as swiftly as they had come. She jumped as one came whizzing back at a terrific rate with some scented herbs in his hand which he scattered furiously in every direction to sweeten the air.

Keturah saw her father coming toward the stable, and she quickly hid, trembling, in the straw. Maybe she would get a beating because she was not in bed, she thought.

But Keturah's father was not thinking about her. His inn was full and even his stable was bulging at the seams; yet he had to find room for two more people. One of them, a girl who couldn't have been more than fifteen years of age, was about to have a baby! What a time to choose, the innkeeper thought grimly. There wasn't one single space left in the inn, and his wife was far too busy to help the young lady. Her husband looked as though he couldn't afford to pay for his food even if a spot could be found!

Glancing inside the stable, Keturah's father turned to the young maiden's husband and said, "There's room in that corner stall with the donkey if you like. There is nowhere else." The man began to protest, but the young maid stopped him.

"Joseph, this will do," she said wearily but thankfully. "It's warm and it's better than the field!"

Keturah's father disappeared, and the man and his maid pushed their way into the stable and out of the chill wind that had sprung up. Keturah was frightened. Now she would be found and she would get a whipping.

The young woman, whose name was Mary, saw her first. "Why, Joseph, look!"

"Hello," Joseph said, in a nice, deep voice that made Keturah feel safe at once.

Keturah gazed into Mary's face and smiled a swift, grateful smile. Then she asked, "May I stay here? I promise to be very, very quiet."

Mary nodded yes. Then she bent over and called, "Joseph, hurry, the baby is coming!"

Keturah gasped. The maid was going to have her baby right here and now! Keturah knew her mother was far too busy to come and help her. Whatever would they do?

"I'll go and get some help from the inn," Joseph said, hurrying out the door. Keturah looked anxiously at the maid. She felt so helpless that she hid her hands in the folds of her wide robe.

Keturah felt her heart beating faster with fear. The baby was about to be born and she was going to be there when it happened! What would she do if the man asked her to pour the water, or stroke the maid's hair, or hold the baby?

All through the night the animals in the stables were as still as they could be. But out in the courtyard, the camels seemed to be showing the horses how to kneel. Keturah thought she heard them talking, saying something about having to kneel down when the King came. "I must be dreaming," she said to herself out loud.

The bright star brilliantly lit up everything. Keturah helped Joseph clean out the manger and helped put fresh hay in it. Joseph was very pleased with Keturah's idea of using the manger for a crib and kept saying, "Thank you, Keturah." Few people ever said thank you to her. The little girl was beside herself with joy.

Early in the morning the baby was born. It was funny, really, because Keturah was sure it was morning, yet the stars were still out. She struggled past the animals and went outside and looked above the inn. Then she saw the heavens full of angels suspended in space, making the whole world look white.

Now Keturah was really frightened. Maybe this wasn't a dream! Maybe she really heard the animals talk last night!

She heard Joseph chuckle. Turning around she saw he was helping Mary wrap the newborn baby boy in strips of cloth.

Suddenly shepherds appeared in the doorway. They pushed their way past the rough donkey to Mary. When they saw the baby wrapped in strips of cloth, they fell on their knees and bowed their heads before Him. Keturah listened in amazement as the shepherds told Joseph and Mary their story.

"Angels from heaven came to our hillside as we were keeping watch over our flock," they said. "They told us that Christ had been born in Bethlehem, for us! A Savior! Emmanuel! We came with haste to see if these things were so."

Keturah began to understand a lot of things. She knew the cherubs she thought she had dreamed about had been real. She understood why the bright star was pointing its heavenly finger at the stable, and why the camels were behaving in such a strange way! God was visiting His people!

Creeping around Donkey, Keturah fell on her knees beside the shepherds. She couldn't quite see because her eyes were full of tears. When at last she looked up, the shepherds had gone back to their flocks. In their place knelt three of the most richly dressed men Keturah had ever seen.

"Are you angels, too?" she asked in astonishment. But the men weren't listening to Keturah; they were talking excitedly with Joseph and laying down gifts beside the manger bed. There were jars of sweet frankincense and myrrh and a small chest of gold. Joseph asked one of the kings, "Where have you come from?"

The man replied, "We have seen His star in the east and have come to worship Him."

Keturah couldn't help but interrupt the man and ask her own questions. "Is the star you saw in the east the same one that hangs over our stable?"

The man answered her kindly, saying, "Yes, young maid. The star is very important to us. It tells us that a king is born!"

After the men from the east had gone to rest at the inn, Keturah lay down beside Donkey thinking how amazing it all was.

Keturah's thoughts were interrupted by Mary's voice.

"Keturah, come here," she said. Keturah scrambled off her bed of hay and appeared at Mary's side in an instant.

"Keturah, would you like to hold the baby?" asked Mary gently.

"Hold the baby!" she gasped. "Oh, yes, I'd love to!" But then a great horror swept over her. Mary didn't know she didn't have any fingers. She couldn't hold the baby. She might drop Him.

Mary went back to the rough trough that was serving as a crib and lifted the little Lord Jesus out of it. Then she came back to Keturah who was sitting on the floor, her eyes every bit as bright and shining as the huge star that shone over the stable door.

Placing Jesus in Keturah's arms, Mary returned to Joseph, tired beyond measure. "Put Him back in the manger when you're ready," she said to the little girl as she fell asleep.

Keturah didn't know how long she held the Christ Child. How do you count the moments when God is in your arms? She had never in her life felt as she felt then. Her very soul seemed to be on fire with love and thankfulness. Tears of joy rolled down her cheeks, splashing onto the Baby Jesus' sleeping face, and she hastened to wipe them away.

A cold chill spread over Keturah. She had wiped the tears away! How had she done that? She got up with some difficulty, struggling to stand upright with the baby held tightly against her chest. She walked to the manger and tenderly laid the baby down in the bed of hay. As she straightened up, her eyes slowly fell to her hands. It was true. She had fingers! Ten of them. She stood in a daze for what seemed like an eternity. Then she fell on her knees at the side of the manger.

The baby was awake now. The star shone brighter than ever through the crack in the roof, bathing the stable in the soft, warm light. Trembling, Keturah whispered in holy fear, "Who are you that you can straighten withered hands? Where do you come from, and where are you going? Why have you come to my stable—my home—my world?" There was no answer. Somewhere in the distance the angels were singing. Keturah strained her ears to catch the words.

"Glory to God in the highest," sang the angel choir. "And on earth, peace, goodwill toward men!"

"And toward women," whispered Keturah, "and even toward a little girl with withered hands!"

The Animals' Christmas Tree

Pamela Kennedy

The woodland animals gathered at the foot of a large fir tree. There were worried looks upon their faces.

"Did you see them?" asked the deer.

"What did they want?" twittered the cardinal.

"What will they do?" wondered the squirrel.

Quietly, the animals had watched from their winter hiding places as a group of children had gathered around the fir tree.

Now the children were gone, but they had said they would return.

The owl, who always seemed to know about such things, flapped his wings to draw the attention of the others. "It is clear," he said in his wisest tones, "the children plan to cut down our tree and haul it home for Christmas!"

"What is Christmas?" the animals asked each other.

The owl then told his friends about the holiday and how people like to take trees from the forest and place them in their homes to decorate.

The animals were distressed at the thought of losing their beautiful fir tree.

"Where will I build my nest?" cried the cardinal.

"Where will I hide my babies?" sighed the rabbit.

"Where will I store my nuts?" chattered the chipmunk.

The animals waited sadly for the children to return, then gathered again in secret to watch them chop down the lovely evergreen.

But when the children came back, they were not carrying saws and axes to chop down the tree. Instead they ran to the fir tree with armfuls of garlands and baskets of fruits and vegetables. Singing happily, the children decorated the fir boughs with good things for the forest animals to eat. As they finished their work, the children called, "Merry Christmas, dear friends!" Then the happy children skipped away, leaving their gift of Christmas love for the forest animals.

Make an Animal Christmas Tree

Pamela Kennedy

In winter it is often difficult for small animals and birds to find food. Here are some ways you can help them. Maybe you'd like to make your own Animal Christmas Tree!

- Roll pine cones in peanut butter and then in birdseed, and hang them on a tree branch for the birds.
- String cranberries and popcorn for the birds and squirrels.
- Thread chunks of carrot and apple slices on string and hang them on trees for small animals.
- Tie chunks of stale bread on branches.
- Make garlands of raisins to drape on branches.
- Sprinkle peanuts in the shell on the ground for chipmunks and squirrels.

A Child's Prayer

Francis Thompson

Little Jesus, wast Thou shy
Once, and just so small as I?
And what did it feel like to be
Out of Heaven, and just like me?
Didst Thou sometimes think of there,
And ask where all the angels were?
I should think that I would cry
For my house all made of sky;
I would look about the air,
And wonder where my angels were;
And at waking 'twould distress me—
Not an angel there to dress me!

Hadst Thou ever any toys,
Like us little girls and boys?
And didst Thou play in Heaven with all
The angels, that were not too tall,
With stars for marbles? Did the things
Play "Can you see me?" through their wings?

Didst Thou kneel at night to pray,
And didst Thou join Thy hands, this way?

And did they tire sometimes, being young,
And make the prayer seem very long?
And dost Thou like it best, that we
Should join our hands to pray to Thee?
I used to think, before I knew,
The prayer not said unless we do.
And did Thy Mother at the night
Kiss Thee, and fold the clothes in right?
And didst Thou feel quite good in bed,
Kissed, and sweet, and Thy prayers said?

Thou canst not have forgotten all
That it feels like to be small:
And Thou know'st I cannot pray
To Thee in my father's way—
When Thou wast so little, say,
Couldst Thou talk Thy Father's way?
So, a little Child, come down
And hear a child's tongue like Thy own;
Take me by the hand and walk,
And listen to my baby talk.
To Thy Father show my prayer
(He will look, Thou art so fair),
And say: "O Father, I, Thy Son,
Bring the prayer of a little one."

And He will smile, that children's tongue
Has not changed since Thou wast young!

I Heard the Bells on Christmas Day

Henry Wadsworth Longfellow

I heard the bells on Christmas Day
Their old, familiar carols play,
   And wild and sweet
   The words repeat
Of peace on earth, goodwill to men!

And thought how, as the day had come,
The belfries of all Christendom
   Had rolled along
   The unbroken song
Of peace on earth, goodwill to men!

Till, ringing, singing on its way,
The world revolved from night to day,
   A voice, a chime,
   A chant sublime
Of peace on earth, goodwill to men!

Then pealed the bells more loud and deep:
"God is not dead; nor doth He sleep!
   The wrong shall fail,
   The right prevail,
With peace on earth, goodwill to men!"

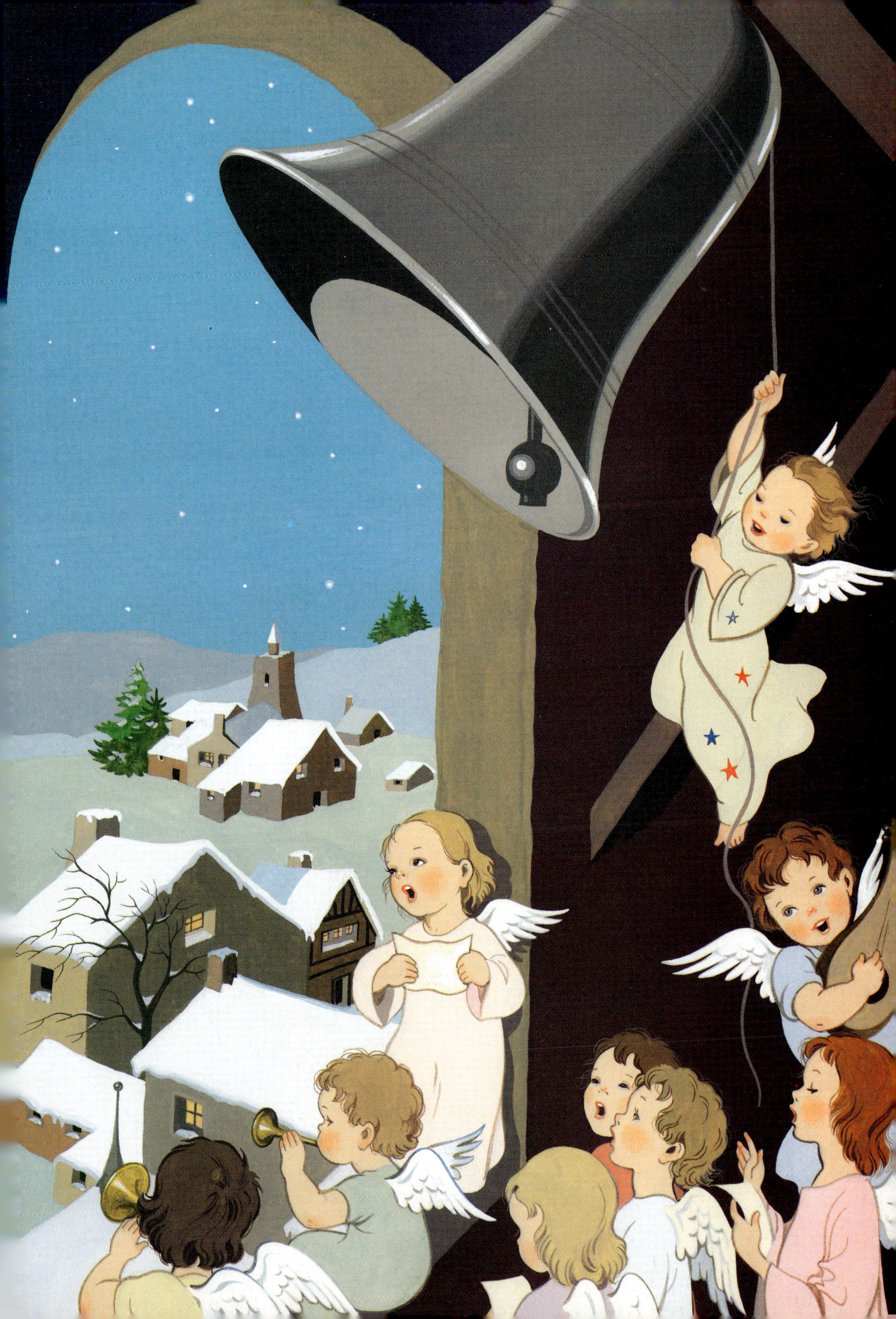

A Christmas Carol

Charles Dickens

Old Scrooge was a tight-fisted man, he was! Why, old Jacob Marley had been dead for seven years, yet Scrooge had not even had Marley's name painted out over the door to the counting house.

Now once upon a time on a cold and foggy Christmas Eve, Scrooge sat counting his money in his counting house. The door to his office was open so he could keep an eye on his clerk, Bob

Cratchit. Poor Bob was wrapped in a long woolen muffler because Scrooge was too stingy to allow him a fire.

With a sudden gust of wind, the door flew open as Scrooge's nephew stepped in to wish his uncle a "Merry Christmas." The only reply from Scrooge was a harsh "Bah humbug!"

Moments after his nephew's departure, the door was pushed open again, and two gentlemen entered.

"Good day, kind sir," said one. "We are raising funds for the poor this Christmas season. What shall I put you down for?"

"Nothing!" replied Scrooge. "It is no concern of mine if these folks are poor."

The two men shook their heads at his angry words and turned to leave.

Scrooge turned to look at his clerk. "I suppose you want all day tomorrow off. You may have it," he said grudgingly, "but you had better be in early the next day."

And with that, Scrooge stomped out the door and headed home.

As Scrooge began to turn the key in his door, he noticed something strange about the big brass knocker on the door. From the center of it glowed a ghostly face, with spectacles upon its forehead. Why, it looked as his old partner, Marley, used to look!

Scrooge's spine tingled and the hair stood up on the back of his neck. As he stared at the ghostly face, it became a knocker again. He dashed into the house and up into his room where he locked the door twice.

As Scrooge sat alone sipping a small bowl of gruel, his mind returned to the knocker. "Humbug!" he said to himself.

No sooner had he said this than strange noises began to sound. And right through the twice-locked door, a ghost appeared—a ghost dressed in Marley's coat and boots, but also wrapped in chains made of keys, cashboxes, and bankbooks!

"Who are you?" Scrooge whispered. "What do you want?"

"Much," said the ghost of Marley. "I lived a wasted and selfish life—caring only about money—and now I must wander like this forever, weighed down by these chains. But you, Ebenezer, have yet a chance to escape my fate.

"You will be haunted," the ghost continued, "by three spirits. Expect the first tomorrow when the clock strikes one. You will see me no more, but remember what I have said."

And with that, the ghost of Jacob Marley slipped out the window into the foggy night air. And Scrooge turned and went straight to bed.

When Scrooge awoke, he heard the clock strike one in the stillness of the night. Suddenly a strange figure stood beside his bed. It had long white hair, but a smooth fair face without a wrinkle. And from its head, a beam of light glowed.

Scrooge clutched his blankets to his chin and asked, "Are you the Spirit whose coming was foretold to me?"

"Yes," it said. "I am the Spirit of

Christmas Past. Rise and walk with me."

They were instantly transported to the office where Scrooge had worked as a young man.

"Why, it's Old Fezziwig!" exclaimed Scrooge.

As he watched, his old boss slapped a younger Scrooge on the back and said, "No more work tonight, it's Christmas Eve. Let's clear the floor and set up for a party."

Watching this delightful scene, Scrooge thought back to yet another Christmas past. He sat beside a young girl whose eyes were filled with tears.

"I cannot marry you, Ebenezer," she said softly, "for you love another more than me."

"There is no one else," argued Scrooge.

"Not someone, but something," she said. "You love your money more than you love me." A single tear ran down her cheek, then she turned and left.

"Spirit," Scrooge cried. "Show me no more. Take me home."

"Come then," the Spirit answered. "My time is short. We must return."

Immediately Scrooge was back in his own room, on his bed in a heavy sleep.

Awaking in the middle of a snore, Scrooge again heard the clock strike one. Looking around, he saw his room; and yet something was strange. The room was not as he remembered.

The walls were hung with holly, and a roaring fire filled the room with light. And heaped on the floor was a steaming, fragrant feast.

Seated amidst this feast was an enormous, laughing giant. "Come in," he boomed. "I am the Spirit of Christmas Present."

He reached his hand toward Scrooge and commanded, "Touch my robe."

Instantly they were transported through the snowy streets to the house of poor Bob Cratchit. It was a simple house, yet filled with life and love.

Tiny Tim, a small, pale child who carried a crutch, sat close to his father. As the Christmas meal drew to a close, Bob raised his cup and said, "A Merry Christmas to us all. God bless us."

"God bless us every one!" cried Tiny Tim.

Bob held his son's small hand in his own, for he loved the child and feared Tiny Tim would not live to see another Christmas.

"Spirit," said Scrooge. "Tell me if Tiny Tim will live."

"I see an empty chair," replied the Spirit. "If these shadows remain unchanged by the future, then the child will die."

When the clock struck again, the Spirit disappeared.

Frightened, Scrooge peered into the darkness around him. He saw a dark and frightening shape moving toward him. Beneath the shadowy hood of the Spirit's robe, two ghostly eyes pierced him with an icy stare.

"Are you the Ghost of Christmas Yet to Come?" he asked.

The Spirit nodded slightly and began to move ahead. Scrooge followed in its shadow.

They came to the home of Bob Cratchit, where they noticed Tiny Tim's empty chair in a corner.

"Oh, Father," cried one of the girls. "What shall we do without our Tiny Tim?"

"We shall not forget him, dear," Bob answered, wiping a tear from his eye. "We shall always remember how kind and patient he was."

Then the Spirit carried Scrooge away to an old weed-choked churchyard. In the deeply carved granite of one of the stones, his name could be read— EBENEZER SCROOGE.

He shrieked, "Oh, hear me, Spirit! Tell me I have hope of changing what you have shown me. I will honor Christmas in my heart and try to keep it all year. Help me change the future as I saw it here!"

He caught the Spirit's hand; but as he did so, it changed into a bedpost—his bedpost.

"I will live in the past, the present, and the future," Scrooge cried joyfully as he climbed out of bed. "Oh, thank you, Jacob Marley. Thank you most sincerely!"

And Ebenezer Scrooge was better than his word. He did it all and even more; and to Tiny Tim, who did not die, he was a second father. He became as good a friend, master, and man as anyone ever knew. From that day on, it was always said that Ebenezer Scrooge knew how to keep Christmas well.

May that be said of each of us. And so, as Tiny Tim observed: God bless us every one!

Old Spanish Carol

Translated by Ruth Sawyer

Shall I tell you who will come
To Bethlehem on Christmas Morn,
Who will kneel them gently down
Before the Lord, newborn?

One small fish from the river,
With scales of red, red gold,
One wild bee from the heather,
One grey lamb from the fold,
One ox from the high pasture,
One black bull from the herd,
One goatling from the far hills,
One white, white bird.

And many children—God give them grace,
Will bring tall candles to light Mary's face.
Shall I tell you who will come
To Bethlehem on Christmas Morn,
Who will kneel them gently down
Before the Lord, newborn?

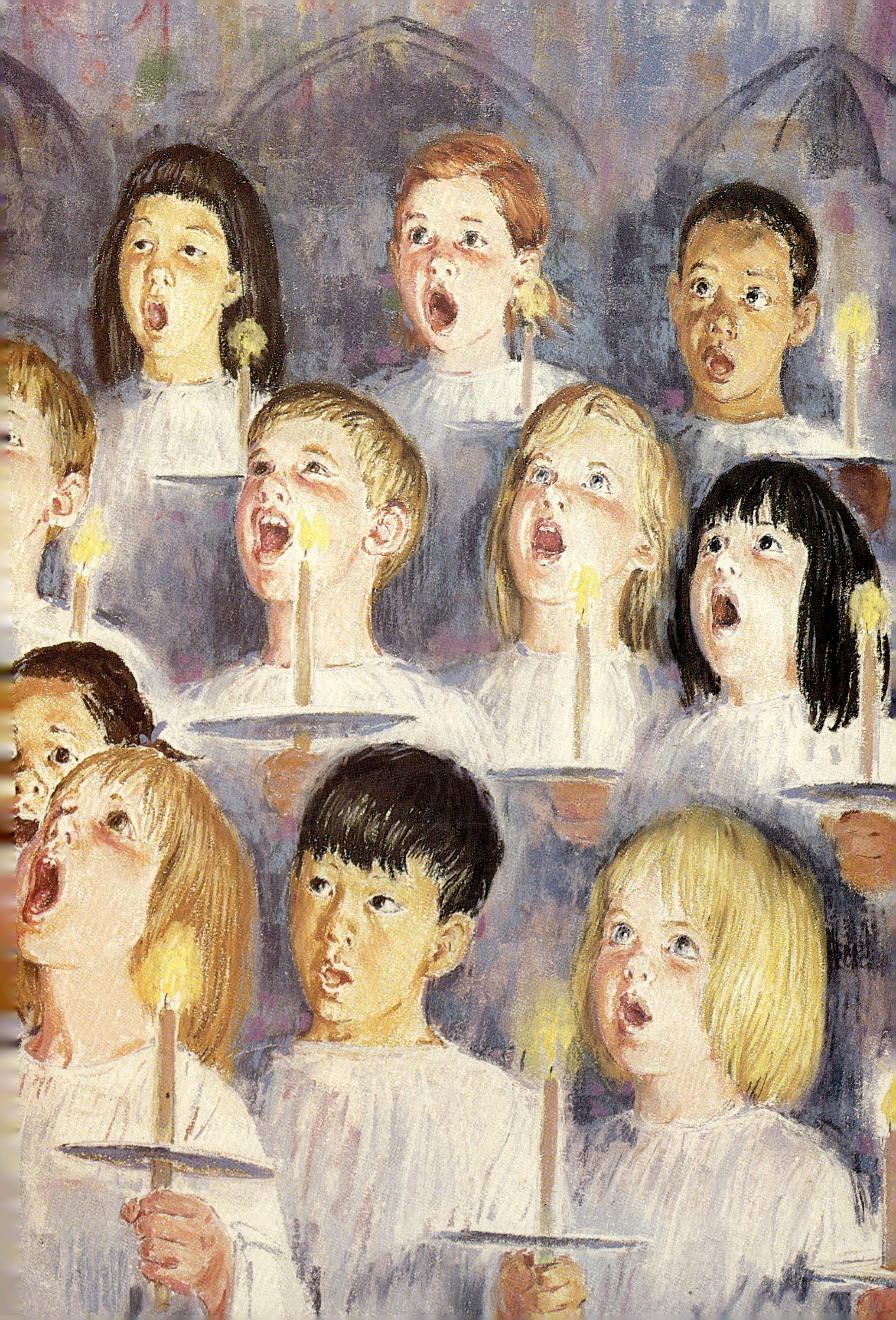

Angels We Have Heard on High

Angels we have heard on high,
Sweetly singing o'er the plains;
And the mountains in reply
Echoing their joyous strains.
Gloria in excelsis Deo,
Gloria in excelsis Deo!

Shepherds, why this jubilee?
Why your joyous songs prolong?
What the gladsome tidings be
Which inspire your heav'nly song?
Gloria in excelsis Deo,
Gloria in excelsis Deo!

Come to Bethlehem and see
Him whose birth the angels sing;
Come adore on bended knee
Christ, the Lord, our newborn King.
Gloria in excelsis Deo,
Gloria in excelsis Deo!

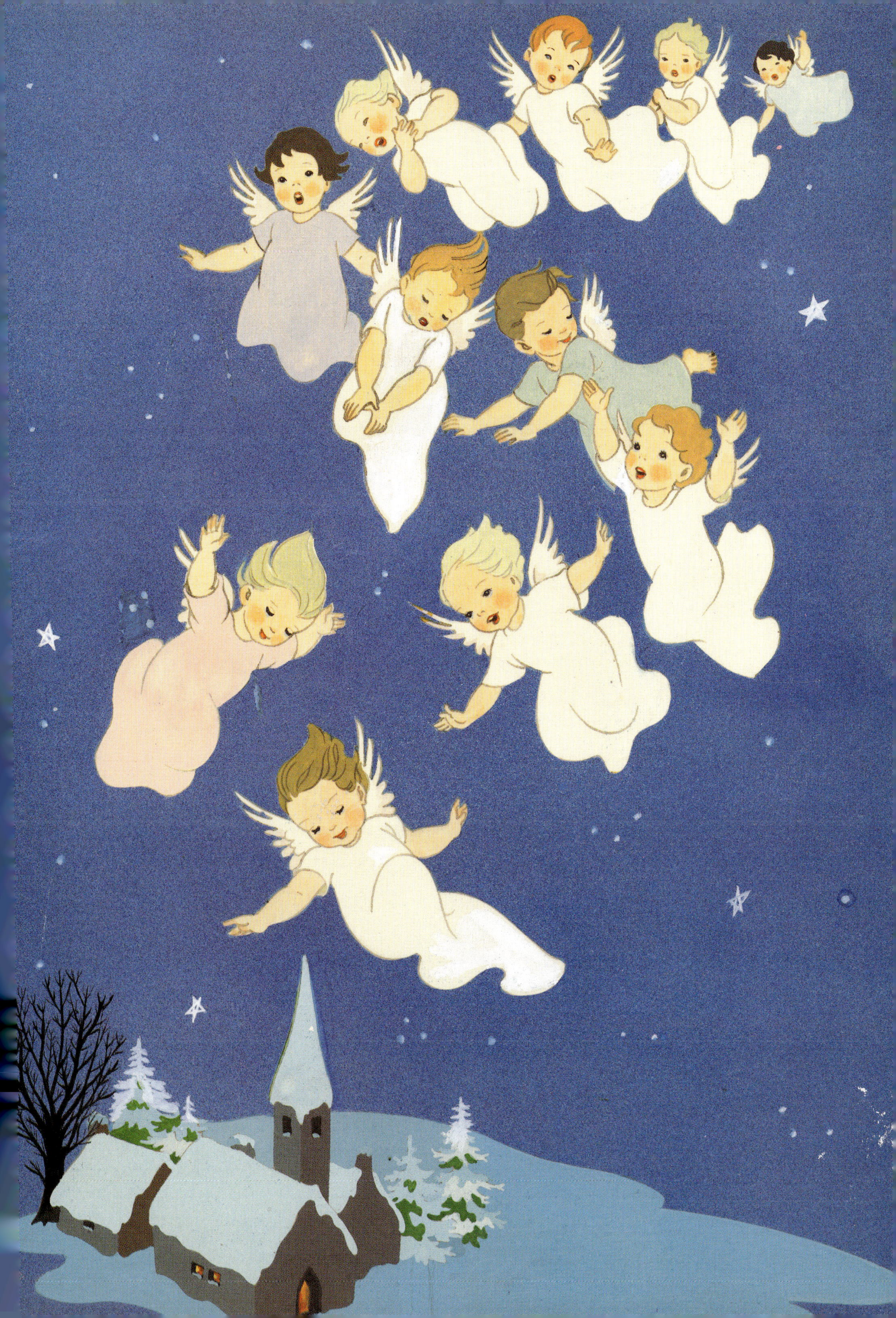

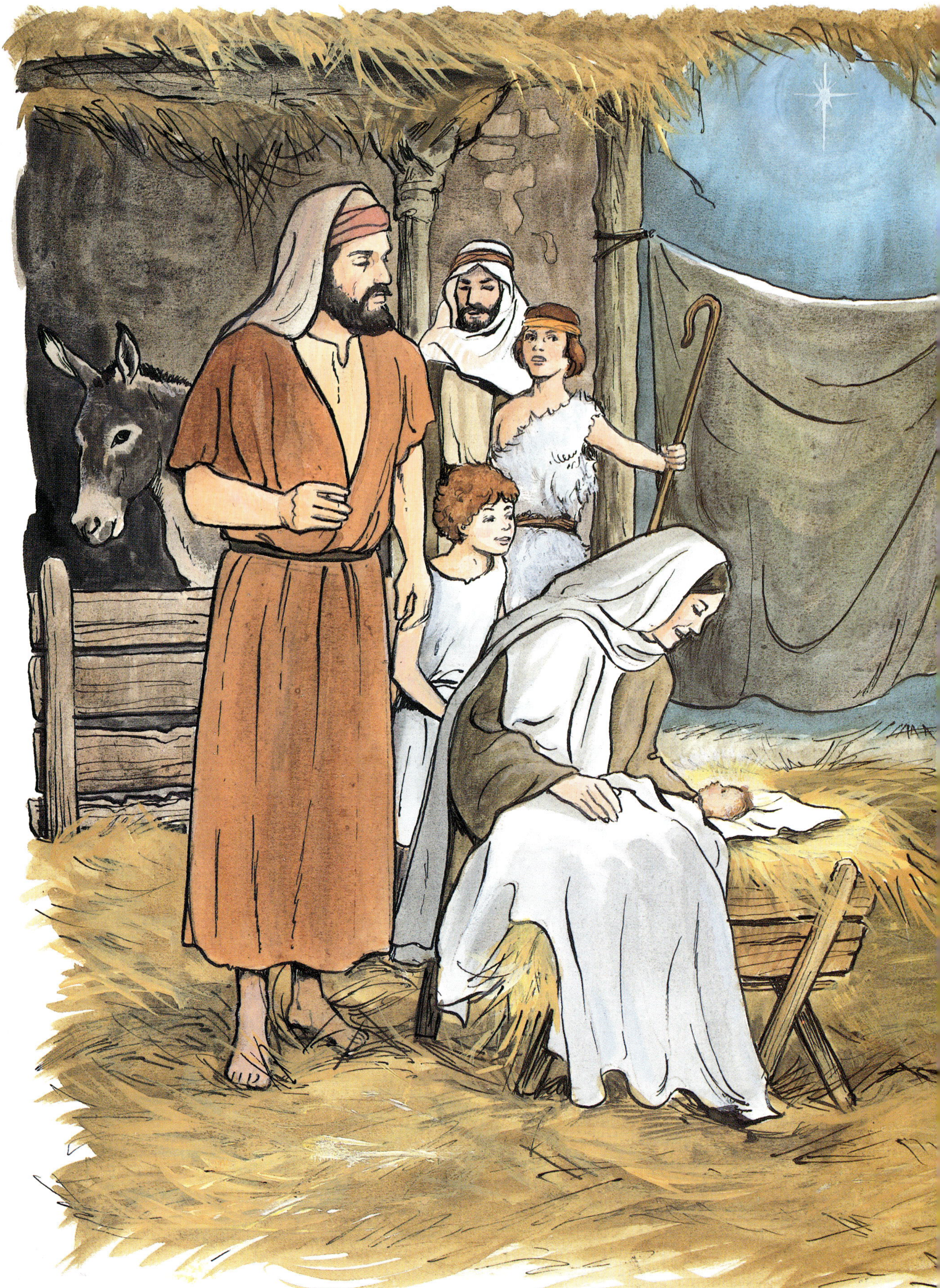

Christmas Song

Eugene Field

Why do bells at Christmas ring?
Why do little children sing?

Once a lovely, shining star,
Seen by shepherds from afar,
Gently moved until its light
Made a manger's cradle bright.

There a darling baby lay,
Pillowed soft upon the hay,
And his mother sang and smiled:
"This is Christ, the holy child."

So the bells for Christmas ring,
So the little children sing.

The Gospel According

"For unto us a child is born, unto us a son is given: and the government shall be upon his shoulder: and his name shall be called Wonderful, Counseller, The mighty God, The everlasting Father, The Prince of Peace."

Isaiah 9:6

And it came to pass in those days, that there went out a decree from Caesar Augustus, that all the world should be taxed. And all went to be taxed, every one into his own city. And Joseph also went up from Galilee, out of the city of Nazareth, into Judaea, unto the city of David, which is called Bethlehem; (because he was of the house and lineage of David:) To be taxed with Mary his espoused wife, being great with child. And so it was, that, while they were there, the days were accomplished that she should be delivered. And she brought forth her firstborn son, and wrapped him in swaddling clothes, and laid him in a manger; because there was no room for them in the inn.

And there were in the same country shepherds abiding in the field, keeping watch over their flock by night. And, lo, the angel of the Lord came upon them, and the glory of the Lord shone round about them: and they were sore afraid. And the angel said unto them, Fear not: for, behold, I bring you good tidings of great joy, which shall be to all people. For unto you is born this day in the city of David a Saviour, which is Christ the Lord. And this shall be a sign unto you; Ye shall find the babe wrapped in swaddling clothes, lying in a manger. And suddenly there was with the angel a multitude of the heavenly host praising God, and saying, Glory to God in the highest, and on earth peace, good will toward men.

And it came to pass, as the angels were gone away from them into heaven, the shepherds said one to another, Let us now go even unto Bethlehem, and see this thing which is come to pass, which the Lord hath made known unto us. And they came with haste, and found Mary, and Joseph, and the babe lying in a manger. And when they had seen it,

to Luke and Matthew

they made known abroad the saying which was told them concerning this child. And all they that heard it wondered at those things which were told them by the shepherds.

Now when Jesus was born in Bethlehem of Judaea in the days of Herod the king, behold, there came wise men from the east to Jerusalem, saying, Where is he that is born King of the Jews? for we have seen his star in the east, and are come to worship him. When Herod the king had heard these things, he was troubled, and all Jerusalem with him. And when he had gathered all the chief priests and scribes of the people together, he demanded of them where Christ should be born. And they said unto him, In Bethlehem of Judaea: for thus it is written by the prophet, And thou Bethlehem, in the land of Juda, art not the least among the princes of Juda: for out of thee shall come a Governor, that shall rule my people Israel.

Then Herod, when he had privily called the wise men, inquired of them diligently what time the star appeared. And he sent them to Bethlehem, and said, Go and search diligently for the young child; and when ye have found him, bring me word again, that I may come and worship him also. When they had heard the king, they departed; and, lo, the star, which they saw in the east, went before them, till it came and stood over where the young child was. When they saw the star, they rejoiced with exceeding great joy.

And when they were come into the house, they saw the young child with Mary his mother, and fell down, and worshipped him: and when they had opened their treasures, they presented unto him gifts: gold, and frankincense, and myrrh. And being warned of God in a dream that they should not return to Herod, they departed into their own country another way. And when they were departed, behold, the angel of the Lord appeareth to Joseph in a dream, saying, Arise, and take the young child and his mother, and flee into Egypt, and be thou there until I bring thee word: for Herod will seek the young child to destroy him. When he arose, he took the young child and his mother by night, and departed into Egypt: And was there until the death of Herod: that it might be fulfilled which was spoken of the Lord by the prophet, saying, Out of Egypt have I called my son.

There's a Song in the Air

Josiah Gilbert Holland

There's a song in the air!
There's a star in the sky!
There's a mother's deep prayer
And a baby's low cry!
And the star rains its fire
While the beautiful sing,
For the manger of Bethlehem
Cradles a King!

There's a tumult of joy
O'er the wonderful birth,
For the Virgin's sweet Boy
Is the Lord of the earth.
Ay! the star rains its fire
While the beautiful sing,
For the manger of Bethlehem
Cradles a King!

We rejoice in the light,
And we echo the song
That comes down through the night
From the heavenly throng.
Ay! we shout to the lovely
Evangel they bring,
And we greet in his cradle
Our Savior and King!

★★★★★★★★

Away in a Manger

Away in a manger,
No crib for His bed,
The little Lord Jesus
Laid down His sweet head.
The stars in the sky,
Looked down where He lay,
The little Lord Jesus
Asleep in the hay.

The cattle are lowing,
The poor Baby wakes,
But little Lord Jesus,
No crying He makes;
I love Thee, Lord Jesus,
Look down from the sky,
And stay by my cradle
Till morning is nigh.